What's So Special About
Dickens?

What's So Special About
Dickens?

MICHAEL ROSEN

illustrated by

SARAH NAYLER

CANDLEWICK PRESS

Second U.S. edition 2018
Originally published as *Dickens: His Work and His World*

Library of Congress Catalog Card Number pending
ISBN 978-0-7636-9992-5 (hardcover)
ISBN 978-0-7636-9993-2 (paperback)

17 18 19 20 21 22 BVG 10 9 8 7 6 5 4 3 2 1

Printed in Berryville, VA, U.S.A.

This book was typeset in ITC Usherwood.
The illustrations were done in pen and ink.

Candlewick Press
99 Dover Street
Somerville, Massachusetts 02144

visit us at www.candlewick.com

Contents

The Tour

A man with a beard, his hair thinning on top but bushy at the sides, stands on a stage. He is performing in a hall in Washington, D.C. In the audience is the president of the United States, Andrew Johnson. There are some books on a little table to one side, but the man doing the show doesn't have to look at them — he knows all the words. He is acting out stories, famous stories that he himself has written, stories that have been read by millions of people. This one-man show that he's doing is one he's put on many times before — all over England, Ireland, and the United States.

One moment he acts out one character, the next he changes his voice and becomes someone else. So one second he's Scrooge, the mean old miser from *A Christmas Carol.* "Will you not speak to me?" he cries out to a ghost. It's the Ghost of Christmas Yet to Come.

The man's face looks anxious, and the audience watches in breathless silence. Later he becomes someone named Mrs. Cratchit, smiling proudly, bringing in a pudding for her family, and the audience erupts into cheers. Then he plays her husband, Bob Cratchit, crying over the death of their son, Tiny Tim, and moans,

"My little, little child! My little child!" The audience falls into painful silence.

This was Charles Dickens the actor, re-creating scenes from a book he had written. He was very good at playing with his audience's feelings, so when one of his characters says, "It's your Uncle Scro-o-o-o-oge!" he would draw the word out in a blood-curdling way. An American writer noticed the way he was comical one moment, the next savage. He could make his face long or give his eyes a twinkle or roll them about, lifting his eyebrows. When he read the brutal death of Nancy in *Oliver Twist,* he acted out Bill Sikes beating her with a club, as well as Nancy's terrible struggles. Audiences were thrilled and shocked. Dickens wrote: "I should think we had . . . a dozen to twenty ladies taken out stiff and rigid, having fainted."

As you can imagine, Dickens's performances exhausted him. In April 1868, while he was in the United States, he collapsed and had to cancel the rest of the tour. He went home to England, but the following January he was back on the London stage. Now, though, he had trouble pronouncing the names of the characters in his books. He was calling Pickwick "Picnic" or even "Peckwicks." It brought tears to people's eyes and made Dickens cry too as he came out to thank his audience at the end of his very last show in March 1870. Here he was, only fifty-eight years old, physically and mentally a wreck.

"From these garish lights," he said, his voice shaking, "I vanish now forevermore, with a heartfelt, grateful, respectful, affectionate farewell." He left the stage, but the clapping and cheering wouldn't stop. The audience didn't want to say good-bye, and so he came back on, his face wet with tears. He kissed his hand, turned, and was never seen in public again.

Dickens died three months later, on June 9. He was buried in Poets' Corner in London's Westminster Abbey, a final resting place for England's best-known and best-loved writers.

I'm having a grave thought.

CHARLES DICKENS
BORN 7ᵗʰ FEB 1812.
DIED 9ᵗʰ JUN 1870

For two days, thousands of mourners filed past, throwing flowers on the coffin until the open grave was filled to overflowing. It's said that a market girl in Drury Lane who heard that Dickens had died said, "Dickens dead? Then will Father Christmas die too?"

But in a way, Dickens hasn't died. Far from it. If possible, his stories have become even more popular. They've been turned into plays, films, cartoons, musicals, and TV dramas and have been seen all over the world. His characters appear in ads, on postage stamps, and on Christmas cards.

Merry

Bah Humbug

Mr A Christmas
2 Holly Cottages
Rochester
Kent

Listening to a conversation, you might hear a strange phrase like "Please, sir, I want some more" or people talking of strange-sounding places like "the Circumlocution Office" and wonderfully strange-sounding characters like the Artful Dodger, Uriah Heep, Abel Magwitch, Mr. Podsnap, Sim Tappertit, Wackford Squeers, Mrs. Gamp, and Mr. Gradgrind. There's even a word — "Dickensian" — that comes from Charles Dickens's name.

Who are these people, where are these strange places, what is this special word, where do these phrases come from, and why do we so like remembering them?

That's what we're going to find out in this book.

The Life

Great writers aren't often people born into some special family who are very rich or very clever or very lucky. They're not always people who have seen or heard hundreds of amazing or odd things. But a great writer has to be someone who spends a good deal of time watching, listening, and wondering—and a good deal more time telling us about it.

When Charles John Huffam Dickens was born, he found himself in a small second-floor bedroom at the front of a little house in the town of Portsea, on the south coast of England. It was Friday February 7, 1812, and baby Charles had an eighteen-month-old sister, Frances, or Fanny as she was called.

The view from the bedroom window was (and still is!) of a small front garden, but in those days you could also see fields of hay and vegetables, some windmills, and, beyond them, Portsmouth Harbour. The room had no carpets, just bare boards, and at night it was lit with oil lamps and candles.

Charles's mother, who was twenty-three when he was born, was named Elizabeth, and she came from a family of musical-instrument makers. He said that she often sent his sisters and him "into uncontrollable fits of laughter by her funny sayings and inimitable mimicry"— or, as we would say now, doing impressions of people. But there was scandal in her family: not long before Charles was born, Elizabeth's father stole some money from the Navy Pay Office, and when he was found out, he ran away to the Isle of Man.

Charles's father was named John, and he worked for the navy. Nothing special, he was the man who helped do the accounting and keep the records in the office that paid out the seamen's money. But he liked to pretend he was grander than he was. He dressed like a gentleman and spoke with an upper-class accent. Perhaps he was imitating his parents, who had been servants in upper-class people's houses. He was also always, always, always short of money, and always either spending it or borrowing it.

One of the most important things about Charles's childhood was that his family never stayed very long in the same house. Five months after he was born, they moved from that house to another in the same town. Eighteen months later, they moved again, and the first of Charles's six younger brothers and sisters was born. Soon after that, they had to move into lodgings (what we would now call an apartment or a flat) in a house that's still there, in London's West End. It wasn't long before they moved again, to a place on the east coast, Sheerness, and then to the port of Chatham. Chatham seemed a magical place to Charles, aged five. A "dream of chalk, and drawbridges, and mastless ships in a muddy river," he called it. There were tunnels and fields to play in, streets full of poor and maimed soldiers and sailors just back from the wars, and a river for outings where you could sail past boats of all shapes and sizes — even a hospital ship and prison ships — and a dockyard, where ships were built.

Charles's first school was his home and his first teacher was his mother. "I faintly remember her teaching me the alphabet," he said, but after that he went with his older sister, Fanny, to what was called at that time a dame school. An old woman, sitting in a room over a shop where clothes were dyed, tried to teach a small group of children how to read and write. She "ruled the world with the birch," Dickens said, meaning a birch-wood stick that she used to beat the children.

Very soon, young Charles began to read picture books "all about scimitars and slippers and turbans and dwarfs and giants and genii and fairies, and Bluebeards and beanstalks and riches and caverns and forests . . . and all new and all true." He loved "Jack the Giant-Killer" and "Little Red Riding Hood."

As an adult Dickens could still bring to mind images from his childhood books: a bull pulling a bell rope in a nursery rhyme; a Russian peasant in the snow; a ray of light on Cain in the story from the Bible in which Cain kills Abel.

"Different peculiarities of dress, of face, of gait, of manner, were written indelibly on my memory," Dickens wrote later. Verses from poems and hymns, as well as the stories that the family's servants told, went into the little boy's mind too and stayed there — along with memories of flying a kite, seeing the future king ride by in a coach, watching a man with a wooden leg, staring at a line of convicts bound together by chains, and getting into trouble for saying that some paper that looked like marble wasn't real marble!

Dickens was also haunted by one particular image: "It's a figure that I once saw, just after dark, chalked upon a door in a little back lane near a country church. . . . It horrified me . . . it smokes a pipe, and has a big hat with each of its ears sticking out . . . a pair of goggle eyes, and hands like two bunches of carrots." Even when he was a world-famous writer, he would lie awake at night and remember "the running home, the looking behind, the horror of its following me."

Sometimes he was taken by relatives (for what was at that time a huge treat) to the theater in London. On one occasion he saw the famous clown Grimaldi. Near his home was another theater, the Theatre Royal, Rochester, which is still standing today. Dickens called it a "sweet, dingy, shabby little country theatre." Here he saw plays by Shakespeare, like *Macbeth* with its horror and murders, but also comedies, thrillers, and pantomimes. He loved them all, especially the pantomimes, medleys of comic dances, rhymed speeches, and more, with moments of sadness and zaniness, boldness, madness, coarseness, and splendor. In those days, actors also staged extracts from their shows at fairs in the open air, and he adored these too.

At home he played with paper and cardboard theaters, controlling the characters with wires. He would put on plays and do all the voices, moving the little figures on and off the stage. It wasn't long before he was singing and reciting for parties and even standing on the table, singing duets with his sister Fanny at the Mitre Inn in Rochester.

When he was nine, Charles left the dame school and went to a school run by the young son of a Baptist minister. Here he had to recite famous poems, learn grammar, arithmetic, and handwriting, and study the morals of the stories in the Bible. At home, though, he gave himself another kind of education — by reading the books on his father's shelves, like *Robinson Crusoe* and *Gulliver's Travels,* and especially one called *Tales of the Genii* — a version of the *Arabian Nights.* People who knew Dickens as a boy

Your wish is my command

said he used to go up to the top floor of the house while the other children were out playing and pore over books and act out the characters to the audience of furniture in the room. "In all these golden fables," he said later, "there was never gold enough for me. I always wanted more. I saw no reason why there should not be mountains and rivers of gold, instead of paltry little caverns and olive pots." At another time, he said he used to get his revenge on people he disliked by turning them into the bad characters in the books.

So here we see Charles, ten years old, engrossed in books, and then all on his own, acting them out, turning real life into stories, real people into characters in his little plays. But he was often miserable. Some kind of illness, which people today think was connected with his kidneys, slowed him down all through his childhood. It meant he often had to stay in bed and watch others play rather than joining in. A brother and a sister died through illness, so the danger and worry of poor health and the terrible sadness of a child's death were never far from his family's thoughts.

Times at home were far from easy. Though John and Elizabeth went on having children, John spent more money than he earned. This meant that when Charles was ten, the family had to pack up and move to what was then the edge of London, Camden Town. This wasn't the desperately poor, cramped slum-London that appears in many of Dickens's books. It was more like a village with fields and footpaths and no streetlights or buses. Even so, Dickens remembered it as dingy, damp, and dismal, and their house as having a wretched little back garden. His father started becoming much worse-tempered and seemed less interested in him — or so Dickens would say later in life.

Although Charles loved school, his father made him stop going, saying they couldn't afford it. Yet he paid for Charles's older sister, Fanny, to go to the Royal Academy of Music in 1823, where she studied piano, grammar, religious education, arithmetic, and Italian. Charles felt hurt and abandoned. Fanny had been his great friend at school, and now here she was, leaving him. Perhaps he even felt that Fanny was cheating him of what he wanted or should by rights have for himself.

It was at this time that, young as he

was, Charles started wandering the streets of London alone. He would also go with the rest of the family to visit relatives in the industrial parts of London and down by the River Thames. This wasn't just a matter of sightseeing, although the rows of houses, the masts of ships rising above the rooftops, the boatbuilding, and the chain-making all made a strong impression on Dickens. The visits were often a form of begging. His father would go to see relatives and friends to ask them for money, and Charles would find himself taking part in scenes that would later crop up over and over again in his books: poor people trying to make a living; people who were once well off now ruined; better-off people talking to the not-so-well-off.

As the family's money situation wors-
ened, Charles also took part in visits to the
pawnbroker. A pawnbroker is someone who
will give you some money for things you
own that you leave with him. If you can't buy
them back from him a short while later, he
can sell them. What this meant to Charles
was that all the things in his house that he

loved and cared about might sometime soon be sitting in a shop window. Cutlery, books, chairs, and silk handkerchiefs might fetch a few pennies, but their loss made the Dickens family home poorer and poorer.

All this was bad enough, but what happened next was even worse. Just after his twelfth birthday, Charles was sent to work at Warren's Blacking — a factory that made black boot polish. It was right by the muddy, stinking River Thames, "a crazy, tumble-down old house" with "rotten floors and staircase, and the old grey rats swarming down in the cellars, and the sound of their squeaking and scuffling coming up the stairs at all times." It was a place that would appear in one shape or another in many of Dickens's books.

Charles's job was to take a pot full of blacking and cover it first with oily paper, then with blue paper, tie it around with string, and cut the paper close to the string so that it looked neat. Next he had to paste a printed label onto each pot. He walked three miles to the factory, worked for ten and a half hours a day with a lunch break at twelve and a tea break in the late afternoon, and then walked the three miles home. As you read this, you might try to imagine doing this yourself, aged twelve, for six days a week, month after month. You can see why people say that Charles Dickens had his childhood "snatched from him."

A few days after Charles started work at Warren's Blacking, his father was arrested for debt and sent to Marshalsea, a special prison for people who owed money. This meant that the family was broken up. A new scene now appeared in the young boy's life: regular visits to a cold, damp, filthy prison to see his father. Again, try to imagine how strange and difficult this must have been for him. He felt shock and horror, but there was also the shame of falling as low as this. And he couldn't help blaming his parents, a feeling made worse when his mother went to stay with his father in prison and he was sent to live with a woman who lived around the corner.

At Warren's Blacking, Charles's workmates were a mix of orphans and working people's sons. We know from what he said later that he saw himself as superior to these boys, and being with them felt like a humiliation and shame. Yet they were kind to him. When he fell to the floor with one of the fits that his illness brought on, his workmates laid him on the straw on the factory floor, filled some empty blacking pots with hot water, and put them next to his body, close to where the pain was. Charles became friendly with one boy in particular, Bob Fagin, and he was to use his name much later in *Oliver Twist*.

There were some pleasures. His mother would sometimes come to see him at Warren's. He played on the coal barges with his workmates during their breaks. Best of all, though, was the money he earned. The one good thing about his father being bankrupt and in prison was that part of the money Charles got from Warren's was his own to spend. He carefully counted it out into little piles and, whenever he could, he would visit grand eating places, like a beef house on Drury Lane, a tavern on Parliament Street, or a coffee shop in the West End. He would order a meal and a drink, tip the waiter, and stroll back to his room.

It was at this time that Dickens started doing what he would do for the rest of his life: he told stories to the people around him. Some were straight fibs — about how he lived in this or that fancy house. They helped mark him out as different, a young gentleman almost, even though the Dickens family was down practically at the bottom of society. But any dreams he might have had of being as upper-class as the people in the books he had read were now dashed. He was falling into what people today call the poverty trap, a cycle of poverty that you can never get out of. And it depressed and terrified him.

John Dickens didn't stay in prison, but the memory of it remained in Charles's mind. When he was released, he went back to work, and father and son would walk the three miles together down from the suburbs into the city, joining long lines of clerks, office boys, factory workers, servants, and errand boys. And, as the world knows,

Squeak!

POVERTY TRAP

Charles Dickens didn't spend the rest of his life slaving, away in factories, though most of the people he worked with at that time did.

His father found a way of continuing Charles's education. In 1825 he started at Wellington House Academy. It was a school — but not one you would recognize. In one big room, two hundred boys sat on benches laid out in rows. Everything that was taught was memorized and recited. Older boys had to check that the younger children got it right. Much of the writing was done in chalk on a slate. If paper was used, the writing was done with a sharpened feather called a quill. Any mistakes, impudence, impoliteness, or misbehaving were punished with a beating.

Though Dickens would later write about schools as if they weren't much better than prisons, and about schoolteachers as if they weren't much better than torturers, it seems that at Wellington House, Charles had some fun. He and some of his friends formed a club. They wrote and put on plays, recited poems and songs, wrote stories, made scrapbooks, and produced a magazine called *Our Newspaper*. They lent it out to other boys to read and were paid in marbles or pencils.

Here's one of their jokes: "*Lost.* By a boy with a long red nose, and grey eyes, a very bad temper. Whoever has found the same may keep it, as the owner is better without it."

Charles lasted for only two years at this school, as the family hit yet more money problems, and at the age of fifteen Charles Dickens was sent out to work again, this time for a lawyer. He was what we would call today an office assistant. Long before typewriters, photocopiers, and computers, he spent his day copying out papers by hand. He would also act as a runner, or gofer, carrying lawyers' files and documents from one office to another or to clients' houses. The work itself was often dull, but the offices were full of characters from all walks of life, and it wasn't long before Dickens got a name for himself as the boy who could imitate people — the old laundry woman who sniffed powdered tobacco (called snuff), for instance. In the evenings — every evening — Charles went to the theater. This fed into his acts, so that, when asked, he could recite a bit of Shakespeare or sing a popular song. Theaters at this time weren't fancy or just for the upper classes. They were riotous, drunken, dirty, often violent places where every kind of illegal activity was happening. Dickens loved them!

While he worked for the lawyers, the teenage Charles decided to do a bit of extra skills training. He taught himself short-hand—a method of writing down exactly what someone says in a quick code that is later translated into proper English. Anyone who reads a Dickens book is immediately struck by the way people speak. There is real-sounding dialogue; there are people who talk with different accents and expressions. Some of this can be put down to the fact that Charles was a brilliant mimic and actor, but we should also remember that he learned how to write as fast as people spoke.

It was this skill that led him to his next job. At the age of eighteen he advertised himself as a "shorthand writer," and it wasn't long before he was sitting in law courts, scribbling away. Soon after, he took on the same job in Parliament, writing down speeches as the politicians debated the great issues of the day. And he also turned what he saw into "sketches"—accounts of what he heard and what he thought of it. The newspaper he wrote for was what today we might call liberal or left-wing, though what it campaigned for we now take for granted: votes for all, freedom of speech, the end of rule by lords and dukes—in other words, reform. In Dickens's day these were ideas that hadn't been accepted, and he placed himself firmly on the side of the reformers.

In his spare time, Dickens wrote little plays, and his moments of real pleasure came in arranging family gatherings, with shows, music, and recitations. (Fanny, having spent some time at the Royal Academy of Music, could be relied on to produce some good singing and piano playing.) But this kind of fun and games is a long way from the stories that he would later write. So, when did he begin to come up with the kind of writing that would lead to his great novels?

In 1833, at the age of twenty-one, he wrote a short piece called "A Dinner at Poplar Walk." It's a comic story of a family trying to chase money that they think

they're owed from dead relatives — not hard
to imagine what might have inspired that!
"With fear and trembling," Dickens dropped
it into the "dark letter-box in a dark office"
of the *Monthly Magazine*. He didn't hear from
the publication, but when he went to buy

the next issue, printed for all to read was "A Dinner at Poplar Walk." As he walked down to Parliament, his eyes were "so dimmed with joy and pride" that he could hardly stand looking at the street or the reality of the world around him.

Over the next few months, he wrote eight more stories, all published, none of which earned him any money. They were all funny, often laughing at the people who inhabited the same walk of life as Charles and his parents—that of the lower middle class.

Next step for Charles was working for a much better, bigger paper than the *Monthly Magazine*—the famous *Morning Chronicle*. He was its parliamentary sketch writer but also a theater reviewer and reporter on

election campaigns, dinners, public meetings, and the like. This meant traveling all
over the country, writing enormous amounts
at great speed about things almost as they
happened. For the first time, he saw life all
over England, life on the road, life in the
industrial north. Soon he was writing other
kinds of articles: comic, witty, or punchy
commentaries on topical subjects. He was
the forerunner of the columnist in today's
newspapers. But even as he was rushing into
this new venture, his father was in trouble
again. And as the law was preparing to cart
John Dickens back off to prison, Charles was
writing stories full of descriptions of debtors'
lockups.

He was building quite a reputation for
conjuring up in his articles the London he

saw and heard. Snatches of conversation appeared alongside descriptions of the poor, the rich, the crowds, the pleasure gardens, the fairs, the slum tenements. In 1836 all these articles and sketches were published in a book, *Sketches by Boz,* with pictures by the most famous illustrator of the day, George Cruikshank. Charles Dickens was beginning to make his mark.

What happened next, though, was a piece of work that would change the way stories were written. Dickens produced a monthly tale about a group of friends. Each month, people could buy for a shilling the next installment, building it into a full-length novel. This was the beginning of what came to be his main method of writing, and one of the most exciting things about his work:

the chapter-by-chapter unfolding of events, each chapter leading us up to the edge of a cliff but not taking us over it. It was the beginning of a kind of storytelling we are all familiar with today: the serial, the soap opera that develops day by day, or week by

week, a tale with many characters whose fortunes rise and fall alongside one another. Dickens's first serial book was called *The Pickwick Papers.*

He spent the next thirty years or so writing, editing, and performing. In 1836 he married Catherine Hogarth, the daughter of his employer at the *Morning Chronicle*'s sister paper, the *Evening Chronicle,* and over the course of the next sixteen years became the father of ten children. He seems to have fallen in love with another woman, however, and he separated from his wife in 1858. He died at the age of fifty-eight in 1870.

London

Everyone lives in a particular time and place. But how do the time and place we live in affect us?

If you stop to think about yourself and wonder why you are the way you are, you'll realize that all sorts of things have gone into making the person who is you. First of all, there are the people who've brought you up, who've been with you perhaps since you were born — talking to you; looking after you; sometimes telling you off; and mostly, I hope, trying to be good to you. Their behavior and outlook have had a huge effect on how you think and feel.

What's more, they've set your standard of living. The money they earn has given you the home you live in, the food you eat, the outings and trips you go on, and the clubs you belong to. Often people's outlook is influenced by the amount of money they have and the way they earn it. Someone who works sixteen hours a day, seven days a week, probably has a very different way of looking at the world than someone who never has to work because they're born rich. If someone spends all day looking after people, they might well have a different view of the world than someone who works alone running their own business.

And what about the area you live in? Particular regions, localities, and whole countries have particular customs and traditions. People from the same area talk with a similar accent and language, find the same jokes funny, and share similar memories.

And what of the era you live in? Sometimes people talk about the "sixties" or the "nineties," meaning that what happened in those decades had a special feeling about it. Maybe they were times when a lot changed and new things started to happen, so what people lived through then altered the way they are now.

All in all, we can say that people are greatly affected by their background (their parents and family), by how and where they live, by how they and their parents earn their living, and by the times they live through.

So what was England like in Charles Dickens's lifetime? And, more specifically, what was London like? If I had to use one word to sum it up, I'd say "change." In 1800, twelve years before Dickens was born, there were a million people living and working in London. By the time he was thirty-eight, there were over two million. In fifty years the population had doubled. The city was sucking in hundreds of thousands of people from the countryside who were looking for work, and rows and rows of tiny houses, alleys, and streets were springing up every day. There was a massive upheaval.

In 1829, the illustrator George Cruikshank, whom Dickens worked with, drew a cartoon titled *London Going out of Town,* or *The March of Bricks and Mortar.* It shows an army of robots made of spades, chimney tops, and trays of cement. One carries a sign saying:

This Ground
to be Lett
on a
Building Lease.
Enquire of Mr. Goth,
Brick Maker,
Bricklayers Arms,
Brick Lane,
Brixton.

(He's called Mr. Goth because it was the Goths who destroyed Rome in Roman times.) The robot army is marching on fields full of trees and haystacks that are crying out, "Oh, I am mortarly wounded," and "Our fences I

51

Bricks for sale

ouch!

fear will be found to be no defence against these Barbarians. . . ." "I must leave the field," wails a tree as the robot army comes nearer. A brickmaking kiln is firing a great arch of bricks into the air and onto a haystack while the sky is full of smoke belching out of the chimneys of houses and factories.

Into the middle of all this change, and as part of it, came the railways. Between 1837 and 1863 almost all of London's mainline stations (most of which are still standing today) were built. This meant it became possible for people with money to travel around Britain much more quickly and easily than before. Interestingly enough, though Dickens was a great traveler himself, using every modern means available, in his books people more often than not travel by the old ways. Perhaps he was trying to capture a sense of what the world was like just before the change.

I am mortarly wounded!

Stop!

And what were all the people who came to live in London doing? We can start with Dickens and his family. John Dickens came where the work was and had to stay when he got into debt. His work, you'll remember, was as a clerk — someone who spent all day with a pen in his hand, filling in figures — and Charles too began work as a copy clerk, writing out documents. London was conducting business with people all over the country and throughout the British Empire. Businesses need paper, documents, and files, and before the days of computers this meant thousands of people writing and keeping track of all those bits of paper. So London became the first place in the world that had a large army of clerks working for every kind of business — shops, law firms, and government and local councils.

As we know, John Dickens went to prison because he couldn't pay his debts. But there were other kinds of poor people in London. This was a time long before you could collect welfare if you didn't have a job. If you couldn't find work, you had to beg, borrow, steal, or starve — or, in some situations, go to the workhouse, a kind of part boarding-house, part prison, part labor camp where very poor people were sent. There you would have to do work such as breaking stones or stripping ropes.

Money for old rope

You might not be able to get a job because you were ill, old, pregnant, injured from war wounds, or born disabled, but it might also be because your business or trade was failing and there was no work for you. In London, in Dickens's lifetime, this meant there was an army of the desperately poor, sleeping out in the streets or crammed eight to ten to a room in the shacks and tenements on the east side of the city and along the river.

Between the clerks and the destitute (as these desperately poor people were called) were people who did manual work in the hundreds of factories that were springing up all over the city. And another kind of work also helped swell London's population — domestic labor. People with any money to spare after they had paid the rent and bought food would have servants. Even the Dickens household, often on the verge of ruin, kept servants. So that was another army! An army of servants, errand boys, live-in maids, nannies and nurses, cooks and kitchen maids, boys who looked after the horses, and so on. Often living in their masters' and mistresses' houses, in many cases, these workers were paid next to nothing and had to do whatever they were told. They weren't allowed to marry or date whomever they wanted, and they were thrown out when they became ill or too old or if the family didn't like them. It was intimate work — if you were a servant, you would get to know the people you worked for extremely well. Dickens's writing often looks very closely at people in service and how they were treated.

I've said that London "sucked in" hundreds of thousands of people. Where did they come from? Mostly they came from small towns, villages, and hamlets all over Britain — and that included all of Ireland at this time — as well as from across the British Empire (parts of Africa and India and the

Caribbean). This meant that many of the people in London had lived through the experience of moving there. It wasn't just a matter of travel, but of upheaval, of putting aside one way of life and adopting another. The mind of someone who had made this kind of move would be full of contrasts: "I used to do this; now I do that. My street used to look like that; now it looks like this." These feelings were something Dickens himself experienced, and they figure in his books.

With all these changes — and because of them — came big changes in people's outlook. Dickens lived through a time that bubbled with ideas about new ways to do things. Not long before he was born, two big events sent great waves throughout Britain: the French and American revolutions. These weren't only about wars and executions, but also about what are called "rights." Dickens grew up in and lived through a time when many questions were being asked. Here are some of them: If I am born a lord or a duke, should I have more rights than someone who isn't? Should I be able to run my neighborhood, even run a country, simply because of what family I was born into? Or are all men born equal? If that is the case, should all men have the vote? Even poor men? Are women equal to men? If people *are* born equal, how come some are rich and some poor? Does it have to do with schools and education? Are poor children taught differently from rich children? And if people are equal, does that mean everyone should have the right to say and believe whatever they want? Even people who aren't Christians? When we say that everyone is equal, does that include people with dark skin? Does that mean slaves should be freed? (Dickens certainly thought so.)

But people didn't just *ask* these kinds of questions. They set up clubs, associations, and organizations to promote their views. They wrote books and printed posters and leaflets. They had meetings and marches. Sometimes there were rebellions. Wherever Dickens went in the country, especially in the 1840s, when he was in his thirties, there was talk as never before about rights for all. People wondered whether there would be a revolution in Britain as there had been in France and America. Indeed, in 1848, the Chartists, a group of working people who wanted the most change, marched on London. They were protesting about voting: they wanted votes for all, votes for Parliament every year, and so on.

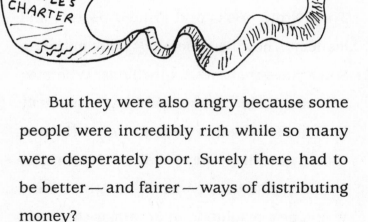

But they were also angry because some people were incredibly rich while so many were desperately poor. Surely there had to be better — and fairer — ways of distributing money?

These arguments were going on as

Dickens was writing. It's important to realize that his books, which show so cleverly and brilliantly how people lived, and what their feelings were, were a way of joining in the great debates of the day. They are, if you like, contributions to the talk, arguments, and demands for change. But when we read them, it's not easy to say that this or that book shows he definitely believed this or that — though when *Hard Times* was published in 1854, it was criticized for being full of "sullen socialism." What we *do* know is that he called for the end to government by lords and dukes and was in favor of more votes for more people. He hated the way the poor were humiliated in the workhouses and the way poor children were taught in schools. The kinds of crimes and misery that go hand in hand with terrible poverty seem to have made him very angry, but they also, quite literally, scared him.

As a young man sitting up in the gallery of the Houses of Parliament, jotting down the exact words that the politicians spoke, and then rushing around the country hearing what they said at election time, Dickens certainly knew how politicians saw things. But mostly he chose not to write about politicians. He was more interested in showing how what they said and did affected the lives of ordinary people. If Parliament thought workhouses and orphanages were a good idea, Dickens says in his stories, "Well, this is what they're like. This is how bad they are." If, as some writers were saying, every man should make his own way in life, doing all he can to climb the ladder of society, Dickens was asking in his books, "What happens if it wrecks his personality and ruins his soul?"

But of course, asking questions is not the same as making up stories. You have to create characters, situations, and scenes. Events have to happen; good and bad things have to come out of people's thoughts and actions. As we've seen, Dickens's own life gave him a rich flow of people and situations, but writers often need a nudge to help them turn what they see, feel, and hear into stories. Quite often they need to read or see some other kind of writing that makes them think, "I could do that! I could write about the things I want to write about in that kind of way." What sort of way was it for Dickens? Well, for one thing, he lived at a time when London had started to talk about itself — in songs, magazines, and shows at the theater, and in little stories called chapbooks that

were sold on the street. Dickens loved
reading about the amazing coincidences,
terrible crimes, and evil goings-on of the
criminal element: the tragic downfall of this
or that person, the wicked ways of Mr. Such-
and-Such, or the highly peculiar behavior of
Mrs. Whatsit.

He saw how much the working people
around him loved reading these stories too,
and so, for most of his life, his own stories

appeared as serials, week by week or month by month, in popular magazines. We call him a novelist and put him in the same group as people who write a book and publish it to be read by a relatively small number of educated men and women, yet really he was part of the world of magazines and chap-books. Because his stories were so good, they were later published as books, and it was Dickens more than any other writer who turned books into things that anyone who knew how to read felt happy to read. Books were no longer just for people cleverer or richer than you.

So Dickens was a man of his time; he became who he was through living and taking part in everything going on around him. But he was also one of the very few this and has, in a way, taught the rest of the world's writers how to do it too. There is a famous story that crowds gathered on the wharf in New York, waiting for the arrival of a magazine to find out if Little Nell, in *The Old Curiosity Shop,* would die.

I'm now going to look at four of Dickens's works: *A Christmas Carol, Oliver Twist, David Copperfield,* and *Great Expectations.* He wrote fifteen novels and countless short stories, but these are the four I thought you might like most. I'll be telling you the plot of the first three, but with the fourth, *Great Expectations,* I'll look in greater detail at how Dickens entices his readers into his stories.

A CHRISTMAS CAROL
(came out in December 1843)

A Christmas Carol is known all around the world. That's partly because Walt Disney made a cartoon based on the story, but there are hundreds of other versions as plays, movies, TV dramas, comic books, and so on.

Ebenezer Scrooge is a miser, someone who hoards money and detests spending it. That's why he hates Christmas, a time when you're supposed to give presents. "Every idiot who goes about with 'Merry Christmas' on his lips," he says, "should be boiled with his own pudding, and buried with a stake of holly through his heart." On Christmas Eve the ghost of Jacob Marley, his old partner in business, visits him, followed by the ghosts of Christmas Past, Christmas Present, and Christmas Yet to Come. Scrooge is shown that because he is so mean, no one will be sorry when he dies. As a result, when he wakes up on

Christmas Day, he's a changed man. Instead of being the old miser everyone knows, he sends a turkey to his clerk, Bob Cratchit, starts giving money to charity, and becomes a jolly old fellow.

Perhaps you know the story so well, it's not much more than a bit of fun for you, and the way it all works out so well can seem a bit sappy. But behind that, some interesting things are going on. Reading the book makes us ask what the point is of going through life being mean and miserable. Is it right that a boss should pay a worker so little, just so that he can be rich? Who in the book knows how to have a really good time? Often in the past, poor people were shown getting drunk, spending their money when they should be saving it, and being generally ignorant. It's interesting that Scrooge, the rich person in this book, has something very important to learn from the poor.

OLIVER TWIST
(came out monthly between January 1837 and March 1839)

Oliver Twist is the name of a boy. He's an orphan who's being brought up in a workhouse. This means that he is treated terribly and cruelly, especially by a man called Bumble, who runs the workhouse. It's while he's there that one of the most famous scenes in English literature happens: Oliver dares to ask for more food!

Life is so horrible for him that he runs away to London, but here he falls in with a gang of child thieves led by a man named

Fagin. In the gang is a burglar named Bill Sikes; his girlfriend, Nancy; and a pickpocket known as the Artful Dodger.

This part of the book is full of adventures, and we wonder if Oliver will stay with the gang or escape from a life of crime. A man named Monks appears on the scene, and he seems very interested in keeping Oliver thieving. The point is that Monks knows Oliver's real background. How this comes out and who tells what to whom is both exciting and terrible because it leads eventually to Bill Sikes murdering Nancy.

Oliver Twist opened many people's eyes to just how horrible life in a workhouse was, especially for children. In it Dickens gave these pauper children, as they're called, a voice, which was important because there was at the time no way, like social media, in which such children could tell the world the story of their lives.

Oliver Twist also shows child crime, which was, in a way, a dangerous thing to do. Dickens lived at a time when plenty of people thought that such things as crime shouldn't be in books for decent, respectable people. The only way it could be, they thought, was if the author kept saying how bad the criminals were, how they would end up in Hell, how they should go to church to repent or be locked up or executed. Some people felt that *Oliver Twist* made child crime look attractive and exciting, and it worried them.

What do you want to be when you grow up, son?

An Artful Dodger!

But the book became incredibly popular, and, of course, many people realized that Dickens was making a link between the cruel way Oliver is treated by so-called honest, law-abiding people in the first part of the book and the fact that he ends up on the streets stealing things. The story, then, was a way of joining in the talk about what to do with the poor, and what to do about crime. And every night on television, that discussion's still going on, isn't it?

DAVID COPPERFIELD
(came out monthly between May 1849 and November 1850)

David Copperfield is the nearest Dickens came to telling his own life story in one of his novels.

David is born in the country soon after

his father dies. His mother marries again, and David's stepfather, Edward Murdstone, and his sister, Jane Murdstone, are both awful people. David is sent away to school, where we meet a horrible head teacher named Creakle. David makes friends with two boys, Steerforth and Traddles. Steerforth is arrogant and handsome, while Traddles is always in a good mood and gets on with life.

David's mother dies, and Mr. Murdstone sends David — aged nine — to work in a bottle factory in London. He lodges with the Micawber family, who are always short of money yet who always seem to have a good time. But life is just too hard, and he runs away to his Aunt Betsey in Dover.

Now things feel better for David, and

he stays in Betsey Trotwood's house with a man people call a lunatic because he says he keeps getting interrupted by the head of King Charles — who was executed in 1649!

At the next house he stays in, which belongs to a lawyer named Mr. Wickfield, David meets Agnes, the lawyer's daughter.

May I interrupt?

He goes to work for another lawyer and meets up again with Steerforth. Another series of events then happens involving the Peggotty family in Yarmouth. Steerforth gets their little girl Em'ly to break off her engagement and run away with him, and this leads to desperate unhappiness for many people until Steerforth drowns.

David marries a woman named Dora and becomes a famous writer. Dora doesn't live long, and David realizes that Agnes is the one he should have married, but by now her father, Mr. Wickfield, is being tricked by a man named Uriah Heep, who is after Agnes as well. I won't say how it all works out in the end.

As you can see, this is a huge, rambling story (or stories), more like a soap opera than the other books we've looked at. There is a constant to-ing and fro-ing of good and bad among the different groups of people in the story. Cruelty and kindness sit side by side, as people secretly plot against others who have no idea what's going on. In fact, all through the book, there are things that we know that a character in the story doesn't know. And yet we don't know how each scene is going to finish, whether the bad person will come to a bad end or get away with it.

All this makes *David Copperfield* a gripping read. One moment we're part of a secret, seeing how this or that person is plotting against someone else, and the next we're surprised by how things turn out. It's a bit like that for David too, just as it is for us in real life.

David Copperfield is a book that takes us from the countryside to London and back to the countryside, and it takes us traveling abroad when Em'ly's father goes looking for her. It takes us from life among the very poor to life among the well-off. It takes us deep into family loyalty and contrasts it with the way people can mistreat their stepchildren. It shows us people who live by the law and have a very strong sense of right and wrong, and others who break all the rules and don't care whom they hurt. It shows us crazy people, characters who aren't crazy, and someone who is nearly driven crazy. And, at the end of the book, we see how the people of England don't live only in England. They're now going "out to the Colonies"— working and making money in the British Empire.

All this is why *David Copperfield* isn't only a book about people. It's a book about society. That means it's a book about how the different parts of a country are living. By getting us to care about what happens to people in the story, Dickens gets us to think about what is a good or a bad way to behave. He shows us how hard it is for good people to stop bad people from harming them and how easy it is not to realize what's going on.

GREAT EXPECTATIONS
(came out weekly between December 1860 and August 1861)

In some ways, *Great Expectations* is a bit like *David Copperfield,* as it tells the story of a boy growing into a man and trying to make his way in life. Pip is brought up by his sister and her kind husband, Joe, a village blacksmith. He gets to know a very wealthy woman named Miss Havisham, who was deserted by her husband-to-be on the day of her wedding. She is bringing up a girl named Estella and teaching her to be cruel to men as a strange kind of revenge.

Pip starts to have ideas that he can become a "gentleman," and not a "common labouring-boy." This is because he's told he's going to come in to some money when he's older. He assumes that it'll be coming from Miss Havisham and promptly deserts and shuns Joe, who has looked after him and loved him.

In fact, Pip has got a lot of things wrong — almost everything! Miss Havisham isn't the one who's left him the money, and her stepdaughter, Estella, whom Pip adores and hopes to marry, treats him badly and goes off with someone else.

Great Expectations is a story that gets us thinking about what it means to turn your back on people who love you, and what it means to be kind and unkind. By getting close to one character, Pip, we see how longing to turn yourself into a gentleman might easily cause you and others close to you to suffer. Interestingly, most of the people in the book who are of the "gentle" class, or upper-middle class, as we might say today, are neither nice nor gentle! And because the book shows one person changing and evolving, it helps us think about whether human beings will always be the way they were born — or whether they can change.

Like all of Dickens's books, it is full of stunning moments. This is partly because the person telling the story, Pip himself, has to admit over and over again that he keeps getting things wrong. This makes him an antihero — in fact, he's one of the first ever to be found in books.

An antihero is someone who is the main character, the one we care about and are most interested in, but instead of being clever or brave or good and right, the character is

Can I have your autograph, Pip?

weak, imperfect, often wrong, and sometimes bad. Up until *Great Expectations,* there
had been heroes who were rascals and
thieves, even villains, but they were always
lovable and often in some way or another a
victim. What makes Pip more of an antihero
is that he isn't a victim. If bad things happen
to him, it's mostly his fault. The only way he

becomes anything like a hero is in the way he comes to realize where he's gone wrong.

All this makes *Great Expectations* a very special book. Instead of being what we might call romantic and working out all right in the end, it shows us something more real than that. It lets us see what it feels like to be weak and not well meaning or well intentioned. It doesn't give us an easy, warm feeling. Indeed, one of Dickens's friends was so upset that the story seemed to finish without a happy ending, he made him write a new ending in which things do look like they'll work out all right for Pip. I think that the first ending Dickens came up with was a better way for the book to finish. Plenty of us don't get everything right in life, and events don't always work out nice and neatly for us. Every now and then, why not have a book that runs against the tide of neat, happy endings and shows us life as it is?

As we have seen, *Great Expectations* tells the story of Pip, an orphan who is being brought up by his older sister and her husband, Joe. Mrs. Joe, as Pip calls her, is a tough parent to her young brother. But the very first chapter shows us something even tougher. In it Dickens creates a scene that is full of terror and lays over that a sense of mystery. It's part of what makes him such a powerful writer. Pip is walking in a graveyard when he is seized by someone who shouts, "Keep still, you little devil, or I'll cut your throat!" It turns out to be a convict who's escaped from a prison ship moored nearby. He's named Magwitch, and this isn't the only time in the book that he surprises us. In fact, he is the surprise of the whole book, but I don't want to give the plot away and tell you how. At this moment of terror, he wants Pip to bring him some food and a rasp, so that he can file off the bit of chain around his leg. It's just before Pip and his family are going to have their Christmas dinner, and Pip steals some food and drink for Magwitch.

The Christmas dinner scene is agonizing as Mrs. Joe goes to serve up a drink that Pip has stolen and swapped with a horrible medicine called tar-water, and then looks for a pie that he has given to Magwitch. It's agonizing partly because Mrs. Joe is very scary, but also because someone is there who is just a little better off than Pip's family.

He is Joe's Uncle Pumblechook (though

Mrs. Joe seems rather more fond of him than her husband does). He's "a large hard-breathing middle-aged slow man, with a mouth like a fish, dull staring eyes, and sandy hair standing upright on his head, so that he looked as if he had just been all but choked." And next thing, in the story, Pumblechook does indeed choke when he drinks the tar-water! Pip only gets out of what would have been terrible trouble when soldiers capture Magwitch, and he tells them that *he* stole the food and drink. Close call!

This is typical Dickens: a scene where we know more than some of the key characters. When Mrs. Joe goes out to get the drink, we know, like Pip, that it's tar-water, so we share his agony. It becomes our agony. What happens to Pip matters to us. This is what we mean when we say that a writer engages our sympathy, and no one does it better than Dickens. We worry that Pip will be in terrible trouble. We see that dangerous and frightening things are going on "out there," and that at home things aren't too safe either.

One day, Mrs. Joe comes back from the market with Uncle Pumblechook and says to Joe, "If this boy ain't grateful this night, he never will be!" The news is that Miss Havisham from uptown wants Pip to go and play at her house. Pip takes up the story: "I had heard of Miss Havisham up town — everybody for miles round had heard of Miss Havisham up town — as an immensely rich and grim lady who lived in a large and dismal house barricaded against robbers, and who led a life of seclusion."

We hear that Uncle Pumblechook has recommended Pip to her. How we learn this is one of the many moments in *Great Expectations* that can best be described as uncomfortable. Mrs. Joe is not only terrifying and hard on her little brother, she is also a snob. She is a snob toward people she thinks are beneath her, and that includes her husband, a kind, loving, and utterly decent man. And she grovels before people she thinks of as above her, like Uncle Pumblechook and Miss Havisham.

This is how she explains the situation to Joe:

"And couldn't Uncle Pumblechook, being always considerate and thoughtful for us — though you may not think it, Joseph," in a tone of the deepest reproach, as if he were the most callous of nephews, "then mention this boy, standing Prancing here"— which I solemnly declare I was not doing —"that I have for ever been a willing slave to?"

Here you see Mrs. Joe rushing through her thoughts and words, only half making sense, trying to say everything at once, and showing herself to be snobbish and groveling, and horrible to Pip, all at the same time! And the whole thing is conveyed in what someone is saying: Dickens reveals what Mrs. Joe is thinking even though she may not know that it's what she's thinking herself!

Going to see Miss Havisham means that Pip must be cleaned up, as Mrs. Joe says that he is "grimed with crock and dirt from the hair of his head to the sole of his foot!" ("Crock" is dye rubbed off cheap cloth or leather.) He is pounced on "like an eagle on a lamb," his face "squeezed into wooden bowls in sinks," and he is "soaped, and kneaded, and towelled, and thumped, and harrowed, and rasped" until, he says, "I really was quite beside myself."

THIS SOAP GUARANTEES TO WASH OFF ALL TRACES OF LOWLY ORIGINS

WORKING CLASS SOAP

He is put into clean clothes "of the stiffest character . . . trussed up" in his "tightest and fearfullest suit." (By the way, there's no such word as "fearfullest," but Dickens loved to make up words. It was a way of letting the true feelings of a character break through, as if ordinary words weren't quite up to the job.) Here he is working with symbols — that's to say, what we are being shown means something else, suggests something more. Over and over again in *Great Expectations* we see Pip struggling with his feelings of wanting to get on in life, to succeed, to better himself. So this moment of cleaning himself up is not only a matter of trying to clean himself of something dirty, but also symbolic of cleaning himself of his background, washing off something he's ashamed of. At this stage both Pip and we, the readers, are only dimly aware of this.

Anyway, at last Pip is ready to leave. "Boy," says Uncle Pumblechook:

"be for ever grateful to all friends, but espe-cially unto them which brought you up by hand!"

"Good-bye, Joe!"

"God bless you, Pip, old chap!"

You can see here the great difference between Pumblechook and his nephew, Joe, expressed entirely in what they say. The uncle always has to deliver little lessons to Pip, making him feel less than he is, while Joe simply blesses Pip. Pumblechook calls him "boy"; Joe calls him "Pip, old chap!" So Dickens reveals what people are like through the dialogue, as events move on and change.

One way of looking at different people is to see them standing on different rungs of a ladder. By now in *Great Expectations,* Dickens has shown us someone on the very bottom: Abel Magwitch; someone who might be called poor but honest: Joe; someone who thinks she's above that: Mrs. Joe; someone who is a notch above: Uncle Pumblechook; and someone we've heard of but not seen who is much higher still: Miss Havisham. Dickens is especially good at showing people across the whole of society, bumping into one another, in conflict with one another, and moving up and down the ladder — just as he did in his own life, and just as he saw people doing in the world around him.

Pip, as we guess by now, is the person who will be having the "great expectations" of the title. Or, to put it another way, where on the ladder will Pip end up? As he goes off in the little horse and cart, he says that he sees the stars coming out one by one, "without throwing any light on the questions why on earth I was going to play at Miss Havisham's, and what on earth I was expected to play at."

End of chapter!

Here Dickens gives us what is called a cliffhanger. We are left wanting to know what happens next and wondering if there is more going on than meets the eye. This sense of mystery and tension is Dickens's powerful way of telling us that life is full of secrets just waiting to unravel, and in unraveling they change who we think we are. As we sit there after a cliffhanger we are left thinking, Oh, so that's how it is. Well, that changes things, doesn't it? *Now* what's going to happen?

Chapter eight of *Great Expectations* is one of the most amazing chapters in literature.

We begin at Uncle Pumblechook's house, with him quizzing Pip on his times tables in a domineering way. "Seven times nine, boy?" he asks pompously. And all through breakfast, Pumblechook keeps it up: "And four?" "And eight?" "And six?" "And two?" "And ten?"

Here's Dickens creating comedy in a situation in which one person has power over another. For us, the readers, it makes the person being nasty seem rather pathetic, even though the person on the receiving end is still having a bad time. Dickens lets us see how people with power over others are often pretty useless, people who in real life, if we were to come across them, we shouldn't take seriously. More often than not, he does this through the words they use, and the way they repeat themselves or repeat the style in which they speak. Dickens was one of the first to do this in novels (it had been done in plays before), and he helped pave the way for sitcoms with their catchphrases and punch lines.

Uncle Pumblechook's behavior makes Pip uncomfortable — yet again, he feels less than he is. But off they go to Miss Havisham's house, "which was of old brick, and dismal, and had a great many iron bars to it. Some of the windows had been walled up; of those that remained, all the lower were rustily barred."

The girl who comes to meet them is forthright, if not rude. When Pumblechook wonders if Miss Havisham might want to see him too, she cuts in with "Ah! But you see she don't." Pip observes that "she said it so finally and in such an undiscussible way" ("undiscussible" is another one of Dickens's own words, there to express deeply felt emotions and ideas). As they cross the courtyard together, Pip calls the girl "miss" and she calls him "boy," even though, as Pip tells us, they are about the same age. And the conversation is awkward. She has the upper hand and behaves like an unpleasant, bossy schoolteacher, one moment quizzing him, the next lecturing him, the next telling him what to do. Dickens lets us see what kind of person this girl is in quick strokes, all in her own words, as when she snaps at him, "But don't loiter, boy."

And then we are taken again into the
realms of mystery and terror:

We went into the house by a side door — the
great front entrance had two chains across
it outside — and the first thing I noticed was,
that the passages were all dark, and that she
had left a candle burning there. She took it up,
and we went through more passages and up
a staircase, and still it was all dark, and only
the candle lighted us.

You'll remember that Pip was cleaned
up to come here and that Mrs. Joe and Uncle
Pumblechook told him he should be grateful: he was going to meet someone who must
be looked up to and admired and thanked

for taking him on. Instead, he is being led into the dark, into a place where it would be easy to get lost, somewhere that is scary. Is Dickens suggesting here, with another of those symbols, that climbing up the ladder of society is like this? That you may have to go where you will feel alone, uncomfortable, and scared? This is certainly what hits us next:

> At last we came to the door of a room, and she said, "Go in."
>
> I answered, more in shyness than politeness, "After you, miss."
>
> To this, she returned: "Don't be ridiculous, boy; I am not going in." And scornfully walked away, and — what was worse — took the candle with her.

Yes, things *are* getting worse. Here Pip is on the very brink of taking what might be the first step up the ladder, and he is alone, in the dark, and being told that he is "ridiculous." In his own words: "This was very uncomfortable, and I was half afraid."

Pip opens the door, and instead of being comforted, he sees something that makes him feel even worse. With some of the best word painting in all Dickens's writing, we look with Pip's eyes around the room. "No glimpse of daylight was to be seen in it." It's all lit with candles, and by telling us what furniture there is — a lady's dressing table — we realize that Pip is in the grand lady's bedroom, a place where someone who comes from near the bottom of the ladder, like Pip, should never be, unless as a servant.

But, as Pip says, she was "the strangest lady
I have ever seen, or shall ever see":

> *She was dressed in rich materials —*
> *satins, and lace, and silks — all of white. Her*
> *shoes were white. And she had a long white*
> *veil dependent from her hair, and she had*
> *bridal flowers in her hair, but her hair was*
> *white. Some bright jewels sparkled on her*
> *neck and on her hands, and some other*
> *jewels lay sparkling on the table. Dresses, less*
> *splendid than the dress she wore, and half-*
> *packed trunks, were scattered about. She had*
> *not quite finished dressing, for she had but*
> *one shoe on — the other was on the table near*
> *her hand — her veil was but half arranged,*
> *her watch and chain were not put on, and*

some lace for her bosom lay with those

trinkets, and with her handkerchief, and

gloves, and some flowers, and a Prayer-book,

all confusedly heaped about the looking-glass.

It was not in the first moments that I saw

all these things, though I saw more of them

in the first moments than might be supposed.

But, I saw that everything within my view

which ought to be white, had been white long

ago, and had lost its lustre, and was faded

and yellow. I saw that the bride within the

bridal dress had withered like the dress, and

like the flowers, and had no brightness left

but the brightness of her sunken eyes. I saw

that the dress had been put upon the rounded

figure of a young woman, and that the figure

upon which it now hung loose, had shrunk

to skin and bone. Once, I had been taken
to see some ghastly waxwork at the Fair,
representing I know not what impossible
personage lying in state. Once, I had been
taken to one of our old marsh churches to see
a skeleton in the ashes of a rich dress, that
had been dug out of a vault under the church
pavement. Now, waxwork and skeleton

seemed to have dark eyes that moved and looked at me. I should have cried out, if I could.

"Who is it?" said the lady at the table.

Imagine yourself coming across this scene, with your head full of escaped convicts trying to kill you, soldiers capturing convicts, a sister and uncle who boss you around and terrify you and make you feel small, and a girl who makes you uncomfortable.

In these two paragraphs, describing what Pip sees, Dickens actually writes in different ways. The first paragraph is almost entirely made up of what Pip sees. In the second, he takes us back and describes Pip's thoughts and how he was figuring things out then. Pip also begins to tell us what the place reminds him of. The writing goes deeper, from simply showing us what's there and what can be seen to what the person looking is feeling, how they work things out, and even how their past comes into play.

Once again, we might think about symbols. Miss Havisham is very rich and lives in a grand place, and yet she's all decaying, shrinking, and dying. Is this what it's like at the top of the ladder? At this time in Britain, common people were doing all they could to take power away from people at the top of the ladder, and working toward more people having the vote. Is Dickens saying that people at the top are decaying, useless, and, as we shall see, frozen in time?

Next, Miss Havisham makes Pip come close so that she can look at him. She tells him that she's got a broken heart and wants Pip to amuse her by playing in front of her. Pip can't or won't — or both — and mumbles apologies, hoping that it doesn't get him into trouble with Uncle Pumblechook and Mrs. Joe. The writing here is really good at showing the difference between the adult Pip who is telling the story, and Pip the boy. This stops the storytelling from being simple: it gives us two Pips, two voices. It is as if Pip is in a pool swimming and standing on the side watching himself at the same time! This double-voiced storytelling helps Dickens make us think about something that we all do every day: we look back at things that have happened to us, relive them in our minds, and wonder what they meant. Should I or shouldn't I have behaved like that? Why did that person treat me like that? Dickens can be described as a moral writer because he makes us wonder about the rights and wrongs of the way people behave; he's also a psychological writer because he shows us how people do their thinking. Here are the two Pips:

> *I . . . stood looking at Miss Havisham in what I supposed she took for a dogged manner.*

That is Pip looking at himself swimming in a pool, as I've described it. And here he is speaking from the pool itself:

> *"I am very sorry for you, and very sorry I can't play just now. If you complain of me I shall get into trouble with my sister, so I would*

do it if I could; but it's so new here, and so
strange, and so fine — and melancholy —"

This double-voiced storytelling is perhaps one of the most important ways in which *Great Expectations* works on us, and we'll see it at its most powerful in just a minute.

In the next part of the scene, Miss Havisham orders the girl, Estella, to play with Pip. Estella says:

"With this boy! Why, he is a common
labouring-boy!"
I thought I overheard Miss Havisham
answer — only it seemed so unlikely —"Well?
You can break his heart."

What an extraordinary moment! First

of all there is the naked snobbery of Estella, which, if we are on Pip's side in this story, we will feel is really nasty and wrong. Then, unbelievably, we hear Miss Havisham urge Estella on to a piece of pure cruelty. Is this why she has asked Pip to come, so that he can have his heart broken? And is there some ganging up on Pip going on? Mrs. Joe looks up to Pumblechook, who looks up to Miss Havisham, who is intent on ruining Pip. There's certainly a sense of danger.

Well, Pip and Estella play cards, and the game is called Beggar My Neighbor. In a book called *Great Expectations,* is this a joke about going up the ladder? Do you have to make someone else a beggar to become rich? Quite likely, because the very next words we read come from Miss Havisham. "Beggar him," she says to Estella. Something sinister — even vicious — is in the air, an upper-class woman urging her adopted daughter to "beggar" a poor boy who has done no more than come and play for the woman's entertainment! But it's only a game — or is it?

While they play, Pip realizes why the room is like it is: "Everything in the room had stopped, like the watch and the clock, a long time ago." But his thoughts are interrupted by Estella saying with disdain, "He calls the knaves Jacks, this boy! . . . And what coarse hands he has! And what thick boots!"

In comes the adult Pip, the storyteller:

I had never thought of being ashamed of my hands before; but I began to consider them a very indifferent pair. Her contempt was

117

so strong, that it became infectious, and I
caught it.

Here we see the older Pip realizing that
this moment was a turning point in the
younger Pip's life. He says he felt something
he'd never felt before in his life ("ashamed")
and from then on he was different ("I began
to"). And he's describing deep, deep feelings
in the very heart of his being. The younger
Pip is now ashamed of how he speaks, what
he looks like, and who he is. Anyone who
has ever felt even remotely like this knows
that it's a very difficult position to be in. If
you're not happy with who you are, how do
you get through each day? Surely you'll have
to change things: you can discover the good
things about who you are and tell the people

who make you ashamed to leave you alone. Or you can alter all the things about yourself that make you ashamed, and turn yourself into someone you're not ashamed of. What will Pip do? Judging by the older Pip's comment "Her contempt was so strong, that it became infectious, and I caught it"— he is going to try the getting-rid-of-the-stuff-that-makes-you-ashamed route. Will he be able to, or does the old saying "A leopard can't change its spots" mean that he'll fail?

So Dickens gets us thinking. It's almost as if he goes beyond setting his characters a challenge. He sets us a challenge too: does your knowledge of how human beings behave match how *this* human being behaves?

It's clear that Dickens is no fool when

it comes to how people think. Look once again at that sentence: "Her contempt was so strong, that it became infectious, and I caught it." Mostly when people look down on us, it makes us angry. But many of us also feel something quite subtle and, in its way, painful: we notice the contempt, and it annoys us, but part of us becomes contemptuous of the very same thing. For example, someone might criticize your appearance. It makes you angry. You think that the person who said it isn't so great-looking either, but the next thing you know, you're looking in the mirror, thinking that the person who said it was right! You start to feel the same way about yourself as the person who said those horrible things. You've caught it, just like you might catch an illness.

Psychologists have all sorts of names for this. When people like Malcolm X and Julius Lester and other African-American thinkers tried to work out why some black people seemed to accept what white racists said about them, they called it "internalizing the voice of the oppressor." Here Pip shows how when it came to class, he ended up doing just that — feeling the same way about himself as Estella did.

The rest of the chapter shows the older Pip reflecting on all the pain and humiliation he felt at Miss Havisham's, as well as at the hand of Mrs. Joe. But the young Pip can't and won't free himself from the pain, because he is attracted to the very thing that is causing him the pain. He thinks Estella is beautiful and he is starting to want her even as he wants not to be Pip, the "common labouring-boy."

We have come to one of those moments that happen in stories, films, plays, and the like where we want to say to the hero, "Don't do it. Don't go down that path." But of course, another part of us says, "Go down that path. I know it means ruin, but I want to see whether you'll be able to get yourself out of the mess."

There is no one better than Dickens at creating moments like this. They are, if you like, emotional cliffhangers, not simply a matter of wanting to know what happens next, but also of wanting to know what our hero will feel next, what he or she will think are the rights and wrongs of the matter. I reckon that if these moments seem to us complicated and full of difficult choices that we really care about, then we are looking at great writing. I think Dickens achieves exactly this at this moment in *Great Expectations*. If you think so too, from what I've written here, you'll go and read the book. It's much better than simply reading the bits I've chosen and what I've been saying. It's like being taken on a journey that affects the whole of your being.

The Legacy

Charles Dickens became a celebrity. Wherever he went, people wanted to see and hear him. Whenever he wrote stories and articles, people wanted to read what he had to say. He was a success. Whether it made him happy or not is another matter.

Dickens died in 1870. If that seems an unbelievably long time ago, I'll just say to you that I was born in 1946. That means when I was a boy, I knew a few very old people who were children in the last year or so of Dickens's life. So what has happened to his books since then?

Dickens didn't live long enough to see the invention of movies, animations (cartoons), or television. But these kinds of entertainment have gobbled up his works and made hundreds of different shows for us based on his stories. Most people reading this have probably come across at least one of the following: Walt Disney's *Mickey's Christmas Carol* (1983), David Lean's film of *Great Expectations* (1946), or the musical *Oliver!* (first performed in 1963). There have been many, many TV adaptations of his novels as well, which have the advantage of following the pattern of Dickens's way of writing — in parts, separated by time. If they run for six or so episodes, they have the chance to get deep into the detail of the original books.

Some purists don't like these film and TV adaptations. They say that the books were written as books and should be read as books. Anything else is not worth looking at. I'm not in that camp. I think that we live in what is called an "inter-mediate" world. That is to say, we jump from one kind of medium to another — from books to the Internet to newspapers to TV to movies. Nearly everything we read or watch is touched by something that comes to us in another medium. When we go to see a film, we've often read reviews about it in the newspaper or seen interviews with the stars on television. If we read a book, quite often we see something about it on TV, read a review of it online, or see a film version of it first. Everything is commenting on everything else across all the different kinds of media.

So for me Dickens lives in the intermediate world. I've seen his work in the theater, in a cartoon, in a feature film, and many times on TV; I've read his books, I've read books about his books, I've read hundreds of articles and reviews of his books. I've even read articles about the books about his books, and possibly articles about the articles about the books about the books! And as you read what I've written here, you're reading a book about his books too.

The Dickens that Dickens invented is in his books, but the moment those books came out, he became the Dickens other people invented by talking and writing about him, or making new versions of his stories. I hope that what you have read here will send you back to the Dickens that Dickens invented, and that you'll find an interest and a pleasure there that will stay with you all your life. I also think it will make seeing all the other Dickenses, in film and on TV and the like, even more enjoyable.

Charles Dickens has become part of our language. In most places in the English-speaking world you can call someone a Scrooge and people will know whom you're referring to. Many people will also know what you're talking about if you mention

Oliver Twist asking for more. "More? Who do you think you are? Oliver Twist?" This means that Dickens invented something mythic or archetypal — a scene or a moment that speaks for millions of other moments in millions of other people's lives. We recognize it as representing something: the nerve of someone daring to challenge his or her superior; the gross and unfair way in which that superior might not let them have something. For a writer, creating one of these mythic moments is a fantastic achievement. It means that he or she has noticed something about how human beings deal with one another that really matters.

Here are some great Dickens phrases and sentences:

"Bah!" said Scrooge. "Humbug!"

"If the Law supposes that . . . the law is a ass—a idiot."

"Teach these boys and girls nothing but Facts. . . . Stick to Facts, sir!"

"Barkis is willin'."

"It was the best of times, it was the worst of times."

"Mr. Squeers . . . had but one eye, and the popular prejudice runs in favour of two."

As I've mentioned before, we've even got the word "Dickensian." My dictionary says it can be used to mean "squalid social or working conditions, like those described in Dickens's novels." Think of a cramped, old-fashioned, musty place, with an old man there checking things off in an ancient book. It's a tribute to the fact that Dickens, more than anyone before or since has done, shows us what goes on in the minds of people who work in shops and offices.

It is also said that Dickens invented

Christmas. The Christmases that are
described in *A Christmas Carol* and his other
books are occasions for eating, drinking,
singing, and having a good time, no matter
what difficulties or sadnesses may come
before or after. In writing them, Dickens took

what was already happening in some places and gave it a mythic feel, so that people who read his books or saw his shows went away thinking, *I would like to have a Christmas like that.* He lived at a time when many people believed that having too much fun, especially on the birthday of Jesus Christ, was wrong, and there was a struggle between those who thought, "Have a good time," and those who thought, "Stay quiet, stay holy." The fact that Charles Dickens's view of Christmas seems to have won shows how deep into our whole way of life his writing has reached.

1843

• *Martin Chuzzlewit* is published monthly between January 1843 and July 1844.

• *A Christmas Carol* is published in one volume in December.

1844

• Dickens's fifth child, Francis Jeffrey, is born.

• The Dickens family moves to Italy for an extended stay.

1845

• Dickens's sixth child, Alfred D'Orsay Tennyson, is born.

1846

• *Dombey and Son* is published monthly between October 1846 and April 1848.

• The Dickens family visits Switzerland and Paris.

• Edward Lear publishes *A Book of Nonsense.*

• Hans Christian Andersen's stories are first published in English.

• The potato famine in Ireland sends hundreds of thousands of people to America.

1847

• Dickens's seventh child, Sydney Smith Haldimand, is born.

• James Young Simpson, professor of midwifery at Edinburgh University, first uses chloroform in an operation.

• Charlotte Brontë publishes *Jane Eyre,* and Emily Brontë publishes *Wuthering Heights.*

• The Ten Hours Act limits the working day of women and children.

1848

• Dickens's sister Fanny Burnett dies.

• Chartists march on London and deliver to Parliament a petition for reform with 6 million signatures.

- There are revolutions all over Europe.
- Karl Marx and Friedrich Engels write the *Communist Manifesto*.

1849

- *David Copperfield* is published monthly between May 1849 and November 1850.
- Dickens's eighth child, Henry Fielding, is born.

1850

- Dickens's ninth child, Dora Annie, is born.

1851

- Dora Annie and Dickens's father, John, die.
- The Great Exhibition, the first international exhibition of manufactured products, is held in Hyde Park, London. Over 13,000 exhibits are viewed by more than 6 million visitors.
- Herman Melville publishes *Moby-Dick*.

- 23,135 Sunday schools offer free lessons to working-class children.
- The British census reveals that half the population lives in towns.

1852

- *Bleak House* is published monthly between March 1852 and September 1853.
- Dickens's tenth child, Edward Bulwer Lytton, is born.
- Harriet Beecher Stowe publishes *Uncle Tom's Cabin*.

1853

- Dickens tours Italy; he gives his first public reading of *A Christmas Carol* in Birmingham.
- The smallpox vaccination is made compulsory in England.
- The Crimean War begins.

1854

- *Hard Times* is published weekly between April and August.

1855

• *Little Dorrit* is published monthly between December 1855 and June 1857.

• Sir Joseph Bazalgette of the Metropolitan Board of Works submits a plan (completed in 1875) to create adequate sewers in London.

1856

• Dickens buys Gad's Hill Place on the outskirts of Rochester.

1857

• Dickens meets Ellen Ternan.

• Hans Christian Andersen visits Dickens and outstays his welcome.

• The First War of Indian Independence begins.

• Hulk ships, anchored vessels holding prisoners awaiting transportation, come to an end.

• The Matrimonial Causes Act permits men — but not women — to divorce on the grounds of adultery.

1858

• Dickens separates from his wife.

• During the so-called Great Stink of London the smell of the Thames is so bad that a bill is rushed through to construct a massive sewer scheme.

• The British government takes over the rule of India.

1859

• *A Tale of Two Cities* is published weekly between April and November.

• Charles Darwin publishes *On the Origin of Species*.

1860

• *Great Expectations* is published weekly between December 1860 and August 1861.

• Jean J. Lenoir develops the first commercially successful gasoline engine automobile.

1861

• The American Civil War begins.

1863

• Dickens's mother, Elizabeth, and his son Walter die.

• The first London underground railway (subway) is completed.

• Charles Kingsley publishes *The Water-Babies.*

1864

• *Our Mutual Friend* is published monthly between May 1864 and November 1865.

• A Factory Act makes unhealthy conditions in factories illegal.

1865

• Dickens is involved in the Staplehurst railway crash and suffers permanent shock.

• Elizabeth Garrett Anderson becomes the first licensed female doctor in Britain.

• U.S. president Abraham Lincoln is assassinated.

• Lewis Carroll publishes *Alice in Wonderland.*

1866

• The first transatlantic undersea cable is completed, enabling telegraphs to be sent between Europe and America.

1867

• Dickens tours America for the second time.

• The Second Reform Act increases the British electorate.

1868

• Dickens returns to England and tours.

• The Trades Union Congress is founded.

• Louisa May Alcott publishes *Little Women.*

1869

- **Doctors order Dickens to discontinue his readings.**
- The Suez Canal is opened.
- Imprisonment for debt is abolished.

1870

- *The Mystery of Edwin Drood* is published monthly between April and September but is unfinished.
- **Dickens gives his last public reading on March 15.**
- **Dickens dies on June 9.**
- The First Elementary Education Act makes school attendance until the age of 12 compulsory.

Index

Selected Bibliography

Ackroyd, Peter. *Dickens: Public Life and Private Passion.* London: BBC, 2002.

Barker, Felix, and Peter Jackson. *London: 2000 Years of a City and Its People.* London: Cassell, 1974.

Kassman, John. *Introducing Dickens.* London: Unwin Hyman, 1988.

Leavis, F. R., and Q. D. Leavis. *Dickens: The Novelist.* London: Faber and Faber, 2008.

Wilson, A. N. *The Victorians.* New York: W. W. Norton, 2003.

Further Reading

James, Elizabeth. *Charles Dickens.* New York: Oxford University Press, 2004.

Krull, Kathleen. *Lives of the Writers: Comedies, Tragedies (and what the neighbors thought).* Boston: Houghton Mifflin Harcourt, 2014.

Warren, Andrea. *Charles Dickens and the Street Children of London.* Boston: Houghton Mifflin Harcourt Books for Children, 2011.

Wells-Cole, Catherine. *Charles Dickens: England's Most Captivating Storyteller.* Somerville, MA: Templar/Candlewick, 2011.